S U L A

THE SEABIRD-HUNTERS OF LEWIS

The men of Ness who hunted the guga in 1991. From the left: Donald Macfarlane, Norman Macdonald, Kenny Murray, Angus (Bobby) Morrison, John (Dods) Macfarlane, Finlay Morrison, Murdo Campbell, Calum Mackay, Norman (Carrots) Murray and Angus Murdo Gunn.

S U L A

THE SEABIRD-HUNTERS OF LEWIS

Photographs and commentary by

John Beatty

Introduction by Brian Jackman

Michael Joseph

LONDON

MICHAEL JOSEPH LTD

Published by the Penguin Group
27 Wrights Lane, London W8 5TZ, England
Penguin Books USA Inc., 375 Hudson Street, New York, New York 10014, USA
Penguin Books Australia Ltd, Ringwood, Victoria, Australia
Penguin Books Canada Ltd, 10 Alcorn Avenue, Toronto, Ontario, Canada M4V 3B2
Penguin Books (NZ) Ltd, 182–190 Wairau Road, Auckland 10, New Zealand

Penguin Books Ltd, Registered Offices: Harmondsworth, Middlesex, England

First published in Great Britain 1992

Copyright © Photographs and commentary John Beatty 1992
Copyright © Introduction Brian Jackman 1992

Typeset in 11 on 13pt Caledonia by Goodfellow & Egan Ltd, Cambridge
Printed in England by Butler & Tanner Ltd, Frome, Somerset

A CIP catalogue record for this book is available from the British Library

ISBN 0 7181 3634 9

*C*ontents

Acknowledgements

I would like to thank all the men of Ness who with patience and good will allowed me into a private world: Murdo Campbell, Angus Murdo Gunn, Norman Macdonald, Donald Macfarlane, Calum Mackay, Angus (Bobby) Morrison, Finlay Morrison, Kenny Murray, Norman (Carrots) Murray and especially John (Dods) Macfarlane for his constant support and trust.

Thanks to Stuart Dale for not panicking on the midnight tide, and to Margaret and Donald Morrison who carefully guarded the gates on this extraordinary story. Thanks also to Jenny Dereham for listening so enthusiastically, and to Canon UK whose cameras give me such range and confidence.

This book is dedicated to Commun Eachdraidh
The Historical Society in Port of Ness
which preserves the memory of all who venture to Sula Sgeir

Introduction by Brian Jackman

Sula Sgeir is one of the most inhospitable places on earth. A storm-lashed rock, barely half a mile long and ringed by cliffs 200 feet high, it rises from the North Atlantic some forty miles beyond the Isle of Lewis in the Outer Hebrides. Yet every year the men of Ness make the arduous journey from Lewis to Sula Sgeir to gather the strangest harvest. Here, each summer, they risk their lives to hunt the gugas – fat young gannets which are pickled in salt to be eaten during the winter.

These annual voyages to Sula Sgeir – its Gaelic name means Gannet Rock – were born out of long years of need and privation, when all kinds of seabirds were killed and eaten to enable the islanders to survive the harsh northern winters. In bygone centuries, hunting the guga was a necessity; but today, although the birds are greatly prized as a traditional winter treat on Lewis, the expedition itself has acquired the nature of a pilgrimage. Despite the hazards, it has become a ritual of hardship and endurance, a way in which the men of Ness can keep in touch with their Gaelic roots.

The adult gannet is a magnificent bird. With a six-foot wingspan, it glides effortlessly over the waves, looking for sand-eels which are driven towards the surface by voracious mackerel shoals. When fish are spotted, the gannets catch them by crash-diving from heights of up to 100 feet. Their skulls are strengthened to withstand the impact of hitting the water. Their bodies are protected by elastic air sacs and their eyes are placed so as to give a downward as well as a forward view of their prey.

Wanderers of the wide oceans, gannets winter as far away as the coast of West Africa but return in late March to breed in large offshore colonies in the North Atlantic. Of the twenty-eight European gannetries, thirteen are in the British Isles and eight of these are in Scottish waters.

The islanders of Lewis were not alone in their taste for gannets. Even the people of Edinburgh once feasted on gugas which were taken from the Bass Rock in the Firth of Forth. On St Kilda, too, that spectacular group of islands and stacks lying forty miles west of North Uist, not only gannets but puffins, fulmars, guillemots and gulls were eaten, along with the eggs of razorbills, oyster-catchers and eider ducks.

Until their enforced evacuation in August 1930, the St Kildans were the most remote community in the British Isles; and for centuries they had lived off the teeming seabird colonies whose lonely world they shared. On St Kilda, boys could climb almost as soon as they could walk, and from the age of ten would be helping their fathers to take birds and their eggs from the highest cliffs in Britain.

Early photographs of the bird-hunters of St Kilda show them as lean, barefoot men with beards and cloth caps, posing for the camera with their ropes and fowling poles – the long, hand-made rods used for snaring their prey on inaccessible ledges of Stac Lee and Conachair. Although there were sheep and cattle, potatoes and barley on the islands, the community would have starved without the birds. Breakfast for a St Kildan was milk and porridge with a puffin boiled in the oats. The flesh of the puffin was greatly relished and the arrival of the birds in March was eagerly awaited as they returned to breed in their hundreds of thousands on the island of Dun.

For the gugas, or young gannets, they had to wait until later in the summer; and then, as now, most were kept to be eaten in winter. But unlike the gugas taken on Sula Sgeir, the St Kildan birds were air-dried in stone *cleitean* – turf-roofed chambers which allowed the salt sea-wind to pass through but which kept out the rain.

In the eighteenth century, it was reckoned that nearly 20,000 gannets were being taken each year from Stac Lee and Stac an Armin alone. Yet despite these slaughters, St Kilda remains the world's biggest gannetry.

By the beginning of the nineteenth century, the fulmar had begun to replace the gannet as the most sought-after bird on St Kilda. Its flesh was white and surprisingly tasty. Its oil was used to light the islanders' lamps and its feathers provided down for their beds. So important were the birds that, during the nesting season, the cliffs would be roped off to prevent disturbance by sheep or dogs. And in 1869, when the Preservation of Seabirds Act was passed, a special clause was inserted exempting the inhabitants of St Kilda, whose very survival depended on the wild harvest.

When St Kilda was abandoned in 1930, the gannets were left in peace. Only the gannetry on Sula Sgeir was left to provide its annual bounty, although for a few years after the last war the men of Ness also sometimes made what they referred to as 'day raids' to Sule Stack, a six-acre hump of rock lying thirty miles off the north-west coast of Scotland. Today that phrase has a curious, archaic resonance, summoning up older, darker images of the days when the Vikings roamed these northern waters and their kings ruled from Shetland to Thurso and as far west as Dublin. No one knows when gugas were first hunted on Sula Sgeir, but they may well have been harvested since the twelfth century, when Lewismen were still subjects of the kings of Norway.

Unlike the island of North Rona, which lies about twelve miles east by north-east of Sula Sgeir, 'the Rock' as the Nessmen call it, was never permanently inhabited, although it does have the remains of a Dark Age monastic cell, the *Tigh Beannaichte*. At least North Rona's 300 acres provided grazing for a few sheep, which in turn enabled a handful of people to eke out a living there until the last shepherd, Donald MacLeod, the 'King of Rona', left in 1844. But Sula Sgeir had neither soil nor water and was fit only for the birds.

In earlier times, it was said that the greatest prize on Sula Sgeir was the eider duck which provided both meat and wonderfully soft down, but by the eighteenth century the eiders had begun to decline and it was now the plump young gugas that were sought. In those days, the crossing from the Isle of Lewis to the Rock was made in open boats, which then had to be man-handled up the cliffs since there was no safe achorage or landing-place. Even today there are Nessmen who remember making the voyage in an open boat with motor and sail in the 1930s; and one such vessel, the broad-beamed *Jubilee*, with her green-painted hull and tarred planking, can still be seen on Lewis in the little harbour at Skigersta.

Despite the dangers of the voyage, the men of Ness have met with surprisingly few mishaps. In 1800 a crew was marooned on Sula Sgeir for six weeks when their boat was wrecked; and in 1912 a British warship, *HMS Phoenix*, was sent to look for a crew of ten who had sailed from Lewis just before one of the worst storms in living memory. When the *Phoenix* returned having found no sign of the men, it was feared that they must have drowned; imagine the joy, therefore, of the islanders when the crew they had given up for lost sailed home two weeks later with a record haul of gugas. Unable to reach Sula Sgeir in the heavy seas, the men had been forced to ride out the storm in the lee of North Rona. Only when the winds had abated were they able to land and gather the harvest – although why they were never spotted by the Navy remains a mystery.

Since then, apart from the war years between 1939 and 1945, not a summer has passed on Sula Sgeir without a visit from the men of Ness. And in 1954, when it became illegal to harm gannets under the new Protection of Birds Act, a Statutory Order was inserted especially into the Bill, allowing the Nessmen to hold onto tradition and giving them the right to take up to 2,000 birds a year.

Life on the Outer Isles has never been easy. Even today, driving north from Stornoway to the Butt of Lewis, visitors may find the bleakness hard to bear. Here is a landscape stripped to the bone by ice and wind and rain. No trees can survive the constant gales; for the most part, these wild northern approaches offer nothing but an aching desolation of peat hags and heather moors cratered by lochans. And when you stand beside the lighthouse at the Butt of Lewis, watching the huge seas bursting against the cliffs, it comes as no surprise to learn that the dark and obdurate Lewisian gneiss beneath your feet is the oldest rock on earth.

Yet for the 2,000 or more islanders who live here in their scattered communities, this is home, and they love it with a fierce passion. The world is changing, even on this outermost edge of Western Europe. Tourism and television touches everyone, Gaelic remains the first language and the Sabbath is still sacred. Like the smell of burning peat, such things give shape and continuity to island life.

The fishing grounds have been plundered by the big boats from the mainland and abroad, but the men of Ness still put out from their silted harbour each day to catch what is left with long lines and crab pots. Others work as their fathers did; tending crofts, keeping sheep or weaving tweed cloth for the tourists.

And once a year, the ten chosen men slip quietly away on the evening tide, bound for Sula Sgeir, to hunt the guga and keep faith with the past.

1. The Key

Maybe it was the gulls and other seabirds wheeling around the boat which was taking me to St Kilda in June 1991 that suddenly reminded me of a strange story I had heard nearly ten years before when I was working on South Uist in the Hebrides. Then I had been told that a group of men from the Isle of Lewis went every year to a small island somewhere in the Atlantic to catch gannets. I knew that in times gone by that seabirds had been part of the islanders' diet but I had no idea the practice still existed.

Now I wanted to know more so I asked the skipper's mate, who was from North Lewis, if he knew anything about the rumour. 'That's no rumour, lad,' he said. 'It is true.' I pressed him for more information but he wouldn't tell me much apart from the fact that only ten men went each year and that it was a tradition often handed down from father to son. Only if there was a gap in the chain would another man be chosen. I wanted to know how the new person was chosen; he told me that the key to being selected was in the asking – and, in answer to my next question, he told me where I could ask.

A short while later when I was on the Isle of Lewis I did ask and, in doing so, discovered the last vestiges of this extraordinary tradition. In due course, I was invited to meet the elders of the villages and through developing a relationship of confidence with them, they agreed to allow me to join the party in 1991, and to witness and photograph their seabird harvest. The key had unlocked the door to a most amazing adventure.

2. Steer North by East, a Quarter East

I was awoken by silence and a heaving swell; below me I could hear the bilge water glooping rhythmically. An anchor chain rushed and rattled from its locker. For a moment, I felt unable to move from the cramped berth onto which I had wedged myself for the previous terrible six hours. The journey was over so far. I knew because sea-water no longer poured down the central hatch, the discarded oilskins had gone and the thudding diesel engine had ceased. The passage from Port of Ness, some forty miles beyond the Butt of Lewis, on a midnight tide, had stunned me as a violent gale had stormed around us. Giant seas on a south-westerly beam rolled and pitched us across one of the most notorious waters in the world, the north-west approaches of the Atlantic. Out here, buried in the arms of the sea, is a bleached and naked whalebone of rock rising in a spine of sheer cliffs, a forgotten and ancient citadel for seabirds – Sula Sgeir, the Gannet Rock.

I struggled past the wheelhouse out onto the slippery deck of the trawler. Through the gloomy half-light, a high black rock reared over the boat, providing some respite from the sweeping rain and mountainous seas that crashed across the mouth of the creek. Geodha à Phuill Bhàin is the only haven on Sula Sgeir that is safe from a south-westerly. Ravaged by wind and storm and a surging tide, a cave and arch has formed in the cliff and this provided the only landing place. I heard voices from the bow; work had begun. The door of a great secret was opening.

The first documented evidence of the seabird harvest on Sula Sgeir is from Hugh Munro who wrote of it in 1540, and he claimed it had been in existence for two centuries previously. Up until the mid sixteenth century and for a century after that, it is believed that the men's principal quarry was the eider duck for their downy feathers; this is a species that has now all but disappeared from the Rock. As the North Atlantic population of gannets increased at the turn of the nineteenth century, so the trend in harvesting changed. Massive colonies of gannets on St Kilda, Sule Stack and Sula Sgeir were being raided for winter food and feathers. Today, only the gathering on Sula Sgeir remains. Ten men reach back through the twilight of their forefathers with centuries of sea adventures to be retold around the fires in the homes of the Lewis people.

A sturdy punt was lowered overboard and a small landing party, myself included, motored up the neck of the creek. The punt nudged the rock at the landing point. A heavy surge was swelling over the kelp and purple algaes against the cliff. Kenny jumped and clung to the slimy rocks and then nimbly scrambled away from the tide's reach to secure the small boat to a ring set in the rock. In the days before this makefast, supplies were often cast into the sea from the boat to be towed ashore on ropes.

Immediately, work began. Sack upon sack of peats were hurriedly man-handled from the boat and dumped on a dry ledge at the foot of the cliffs. The punt returned again and again with more supplies. Peat to fuel the fires, drinking water in metal barrels, mattresses, tarpaulins, food boxes, tools, a car battery for the radio link and forty sacks of curing salt. All had to be stacked on ledges and notches below the ragged rocky stairway that led to the summit of the island. For four long hours we ferried the supplies. The last to be brought ashore was a makeshift aerial for the radio, fifteen feet long and lashed together with tape. Finally, a tiny rubber dinghy was dragged from the water and lifted up the cliff-face to a ledge thirty feet above the sea. Before the modern days of a trawler drop, the old open twenty-eight footers were hauled out of the sea and wedged in the cliffs sixty feet above the thrashing waves.

Now our chartered trawler pulled anchor, and with a wave from the stern, our link with home and family turned and slid from view into the open ocean.

The swell abated and streamers of sea foam ringed the creek. We sat quietly and reflective as the warm rain guttered down the rocks. Calum, who was this year's cook, had placed a small pile of peats in a cleft and had made a fire on which a shiny new kettle balanced. Mugs of tea appeared and we ate sandwiches from a tin and, resting after the last four arduous hours, we talked in some detail about the events of the next day. Most conversation on the island was in Gaelic but whilst the men enjoyed their privacy, my Englishness caused amusement and soon the warmth of good conversation spread through us all. I was, after all, the first Sassenach ever to witness and photograph this extraordinary and historic event.

Ten men make up a squad for each season's catch. Men from all walks of life in Lewis: joiners, fishermen, weavers, a lighthouse keeper, engineers and an electrician joined together this year in a close-knit team. Between them, they had fathers that had come to the Rock some thirty times. A strong thread of history, friendship and plain team spirit in the face of adversity made this company into a honed and hardworking unit.

Tea over, we spaced ourselves equidistant up the straddling rock and passed supplies ever upward to the top of the island. Four men were detailed to erect the 'chute'. This innovation of more recent years is a wooden structure, thirty-five metres in length and half a metre wide, and nailed together on stout legs and stays. It was to be the vital means to transfer supplies up and down

13

the cliff, and reminded me of a Klondike floom from the gold rush days in the Yukon. The chute grew and grew. Soon a wooden 'dolly' on castors was slotted into place and a hauling line attached. Up came the heavy metal water barrels. Water is precious here since there is no spring on Sula Sgeir. Several years before, a hauling rope snapped and a half-hundredweight barrel catapulted down the cliff, scattering men and provisions. I sensed their cautious handling.

The top of the island is less than 100 metres across. There is no level ground, and from where I stood at the top of the chute, I looked down with incredulity at the whole scene. Above me, through veils of rain, were three beehive-type dwellings about the size of a traditional Inuit igloo. They are thought to have survived the wind, rain and winter storms of two centuries, and each year only receive minimal maintenance. Around the dwellings, a carpet of succulent sea plants clung to the poor, thin, water-logged soil. In every clump of sea spinach nested a fulmar petrel, a fledgling chick in every crevice, under every boulder. From edge to edge, the island was alive with birds.

I stumbled over slippery rocks towards the first bothy where work had begun to make it habitable. Stooping down and searching through the gloom within, I staggered backwards, overwhelmed by the stench of seabird guano. Early-season residents had littered the mud floor with nesting materials, seaweeds, plastic and bones. We duly evicted them and nestled them into new sites amongst the rocks outside. Peat fires were lit in open-hearthed barrels and dragged inside as we attempted to dry the soaking skeleton walls. Over the roof slabs, tarpaulins and visquine sheeting were draped and then held in place by old fish-netting weighted down with stones. A race developed between the three bothies; everyone was in good spirits. Then huge mattresses, which had been hauled up the chute, were lugged in and placed on the wide ledges which ran round the insides of the bothies: these were the beds.

Calum produced a meal of kippers, bread and gallons of tea, and we gathered together in the largest bothy, crouched around the fiery peats. Through the blue smoke, I looked at the smiling faces of the men and thought of their fathers who had gathered around this same meal to talk of work ahead and ventures gone by. They were renewing friendships with each other and, in some way, were reiterating a sense of stewardship for this rock we had come to.

Leaving before anyone else, I made my way through the sleeping birds down to my dark bothy where the peats were still glowing. Within the damp walls, yellowing candlelight flickered on a thousand earwigs scurrying about in the shadows of the stone eaves. The outside world seemed distant now as wind and tide nursed me to restless sleep.

On the midnight tide, we cast off from the harbour, bound for Sula Sgeir.

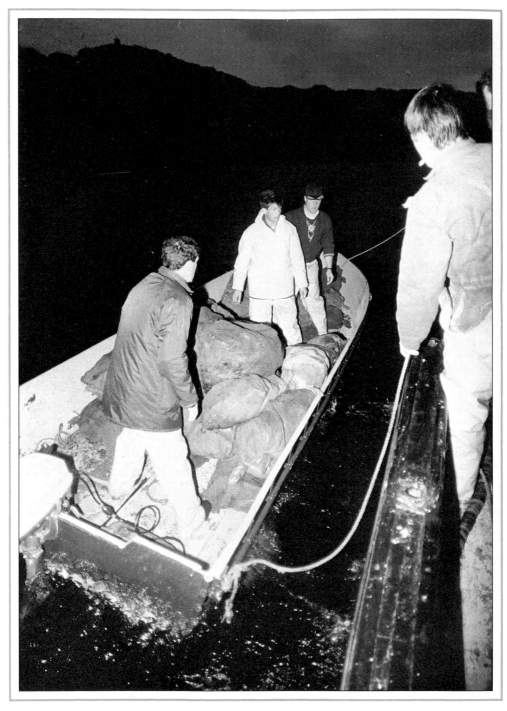

At 4.00 am, during the grey hours of dawn, the transfer starts of supplies, peats and water to the landing point in the sheltered creek of Geodha à Phuill Bhàin.

Work continues for many hours, as endless but essential supplies are transferred from the trawler to the rocks.

Sixty sacks of peats are carried ashore, and dozens of metal barrels of water. Everything is heaped onto ledges waiting to be taken up the rockface.

All small items are man-handled in a human chain up the rocky stairway to the top of the island. Good teamwork is essential.

The chute saves many hours of man-handling equipment to the top of the island. A sea cave has formed at the foot of the rockface, creating a huge arch.

Many years ago, but as recently as 1950, the 28 foot open boats were hauled up from the sea and wedged in the rocks, sometimes 60 feet up, while the men worked on the island. Now, only a rubber dinghy is taken from the water to be used in the case of emergency.

The heavy supplies, once they have been hauled up the chute, are stored in and around the beehive dwellings, the only sheltered places on the wind-swept rock.

Finlay Morrison lifts a sack of peats from the wooden dolly at the top of the chute. The chute is dismantled at the end of the hunt and stored inside a bothy.

To waterproof and windproof each beehive dwelling, plastic sheeting and tarpaulins are laid over the stone roofs. Nesting seabirds are taken from the inside walls and carefully re-sited on the rocks outside. Everyone is required to work on the 'houses', and it soon becomes a race against the foul weather.

Carrots Norman, in the centre, and Norman Macdonald tying pieces of netting whilst Finlay Morrison places stones around the edges.

3. A Blessed Hill

*B*londin, the tight-rope walker, would have enjoyed the busy activity on the first morning proper. A most surprising structure was being erected across all parts of the Rock. The top of the island is extremely difficult and awkward to walk on. Apart from 15,000 pairs of fulmars and more than 30,000 pairs of gannets, the surface is entirely boulder-strewn, requiring balance and deftness that soon became very tiring. Instead of having to carry sackfuls of gugas, young gannets, across the Rock, the squad was building three aerial wireways on which the sacks would be hooked; these were operated by pulleys and saved endless hours of awkward carrying. Each wire cable, a hundred metres long, was spectacularly suspended on crude wooden stanchions and tensioned with a jockey-winch – thus 'Blondin' was the name. Gravity, slide angle and sack weight were being tested and re-tested.

I sat on a comfortable boulder and marvelled at this outlandish innovation. The wind had veered to the north and blustered around the Rock. Below me, I could see all of Sula Sgeir – a mere 600 metres long. The island had an overall colour of black with a collar of green algae, and each of the three promontories was crowned with a white icing of guano that poured down the dark cliffs. Each promontory reared up above the sea like some creature of a Greek myth, buttressing the Atlantic rollers.

I picked a way carefully through the fulmar nests to the summit of a place they called Chapel Promontory. At the turn of the twelfth century, Bruinhilda, the sister of St Ronan, is thought to have built a monastic cell up here; it is known as *Tigh Beannaichte*, the Blessed House. I stood in its ruins out there in the wild wind, and tried to imagine who might have knelt amongst the desolate stones. Bruinhilda did, for sure. They say she perished on Sula Sgeir and was found with a cormorant's nest in her breast. A huge solid cairn of stones marks the place where she lay. During our stay on the Rock, a gannet's wing was placed in the top of the cairn.

All around me were miniature cairns and fingers of rock pointing skyward, leading up to the stuttered skyline to the summit. Each individual cairn was raised in a symbolic gesture by the men of Ness whose annual visits to the Rock were finally over; before each man left Sula Sgeir for the final time, he placed a last symbolic stone or rock on his cairn to denote his former presence on the island.

A chill sea mist gusted through the prickly spine of stones, sending a shiver down my own spine. The place reminded me of something between Passchendaele and Calvary. Then a cloud of gannets rose into the air beyond the summit and I knew that the first hunt was under way. Scrambling hurriedly around the neck of the zawn and climbing the slabby brow of its enclosing walls, I could see the hunting party quite clearly, moving slowly across a dangerous and spectacular section of cliff. With speed yet precision, the two teams of three collected the young gannets, moving inexorably across all accessible grooves, corners and gullies within that particular piece of cliff. John 'Dods' Macfarlane, prominent in his red boiler-suit, led the way for one team. Dods was the unspoken leader of this year's hunt. A remarkable man – dark, quiet, forceful. He had an impish humour and was a tireless worker. Dods was certainly a man to be out here with – it was his nineteenth year on the Rock.

Halting briefly under a large overhang, three men sat quietly gazing out at the sea, rolled a couple of cigarettes and for a moment were lost amongst the dappled colours of strong afternoon light. Close by, clumps of thrift fluttered in the up-draught from the sea. In the yawning space between us, hundreds of gannets and fulmars were riding the eddies in endless circles. Dods and his team moved. They began to ascend the cliff, gathering the birds on their way, fearlessly scrambling up steep and exposed rocks.

The correct selection of gugas is very important since ones too young yield little meat. Identifying the size and age of the bird in the flurry of a kill concerned Dods and Murdo and they concentrated on this single task without any questions. Each of them carried a long pole on the end of which was a sprung metal jaw. Speed was essential. A bird was selected, caught with the pole, lifted across to be killed instantly with a stout stick and then handed on for decapitation. Each team moved through the colony like a pressure wave. Decisive, quick, efficient; there was no pain, fear or anticipation, no emotion, no talking, no questions. It was simply a job that had to be done two thousand times each year.

In just ten minutes, it was finished. That day's kill was over, and already Kenny and Bobby and several of the others were collecting the birds into a heap, ready to be bagged up.

Dods walked towards me with his catching pole and, looking right at me, said with a sigh, 'Well, boy, that's it, that's what we do.' This was said with all the tone of one letting go of a secret. And indeed it was. I looked across at the surviving chicks settling back on their nests and in some ways felt privileged in this primeval scene to have reached through these eons of time and to have seen in the lives of these men a deep connection with ancestry and nature, of stories from the sea, and survival.

Wire cables are erected across the rock to facilitate the transfer of sackfuls of gugas from the colonies to the 'factory' area.

Tigh Beannaichte, the Blessed House, is a roofless ruin on Chapel Promontory in which birds now nest. These are the remains of a 12th-century monastic cell.

Bruinhilda's cairn stands in the axial position of the three promontories of Sula Sgeir, possibly as a memorial to this sister of St Ronan.

The hunters approach the gannet colony on Chapel Promontory. Adult birds fly from the nests and swirl above the cliffs while the men make a first harvest.

In dangerous sections of the cliff, a safety rope is used. Loose and unstable rock, slippery slabs and high winds can make work on the cliffs very hazardous.

Dods Macfarlane reaches across to inaccessible ledges in search of gugas. The men climb into most sections of the cliff during the hunt.

Grooves and steep gullies in the cliffs are often muddy and slippery so ropes are used as a precaution against accident.

Dods Macfarlane has been to Sula Sgeir on each of the past nineteen years. He is a decisive and tireless worker and is this year's unspoken leader of the team.

The fledgling gannet or guga has varying stages of development. The downy chick on the right, though appearing bulky, produces little meat and is generally left to become an adult. The blacker guga on the left is slimmer and stronger, and is about to fly: these birds are difficult to catch. In the centre is the favoured guga or tre-tim (three tufts) and is identified by downy tufts on the head, back and legs. This is the guga most commonly harvested.

4. 'We Catch the Guga'

Nobody moved after breakfast. Many mugs of tea had been drunk. The sheer heat from the peats was enervating. We sat shoulder to shoulder in a circle, thinking our thoughts and wondering whether the rain would ever cease. For two days the island had been still, misty and very, very wet. All the thin soil was now slippery mud, the lichenous rocks and boulders were deathtraps, and we had stumbled in from our bothies in oilskins and heavy boots. The prospect of another hard day was very daunting. Only the crackle and spit of leaking rain through the roof could be heard in our meagre home.

Then Murdo Campbell, a veteran of twenty-two visits to Sula Sgeir, carefully arranged his glasses on his nose, crawled forward on the bed on which he lay and then rose to his knees, allowing the shaft of dim light from the roof-hole to cast on the pages of his tiny tape-bound Gaelic bible. Each day we waited, each day he delivered after every communal meal a reading of psalms in soft and fluid tones. Not strident but wistful rhythmical incantations from an ancient language. I grew to love the melody of the Gaelic tongue. Through the rain outside, we heard with him the cries of wheeling gannets, and with heads bowed, followed their shadows on the earth floor around the fire.

'What to do, what to do,' muttered Dods, breaking the spell, deciding on impulse and out loud that not a moment more must be lost. 'We catch the guga.' Despite the foul weather, we knew we had to work on. Nobody spoke, just struggled for the entrance tunnel and stepped out into the incessant rain to lash up in layers of tattered waterproofs and walk in single file, carrying sticks, poles, knives and sacks to the highest and most dense gannet colony of all.

As we approached, the stench of guano ammonia hit us like a wall set around the birds. The days of recent rain had turned the once hardened mud between the nests into a stinking quagmire, a vile soup of mud, oils and fish offal. Before us now, just fifty metres short of the lighthouse, was a grey squelching bog in which several hundred gannet nests were raised like hapless islands amidst an ocean of filth. Each nest was an entanglement of string, matted together with mud. A single guga paddled about on each one.

Into the sheeting rain rose a thousand gannets as the men moved forward, split into two teams of four. Murdo led a party to clear the cliff edges close to the light; Dods worked towards him across the open top of the rock. They were like well-oiled machines, each movement exact, balanced and rehearsed.

At the end of the sweep, Dods took out his notebook and pencil and, with great precision, counted the tally. He would count at every stage: from the kill to the final delivery back on Lewis. The others arrived and relaxed on the rocks. Throughout the brightening mist appeared Calum, almost luminous yellow in his new oilskins. In his left hand was a black kettle of hot tea, in his right and suspended on a string from each corner was a tomato box containing the mugs. Twice a day, Calum brought tea to our work place, performing a balancing miracle to reach us across the slippery rocks without losing the tea. We chatted and ate slabs of cake.

Kenny and Dods walked to the cliff-edge to discuss a plan for the crowded rocks below the light. A dangerous place on the island, these lower rocks are still high above the sea and very exposed to the blasting winds. The right day ahead had to be chosen for working down there safely.

The rest of the lads cast away their tea leaves, stood up adjusting uncomfortable and clammy clothing, and set to work with few words uttered. Two men went to receive the sacks of birds at the plucking site, the rest bagged up the gugas, and hooked them on to the Blondin line. For twenty minutes, sacks of birds swung along the squeaking wires. A heavy sack descending the wires pulled an empty sack back up but a fault stopped the operation. By slackening the cables, the men were able to move the bags on slowly, but the problem wasn't solved. The wires were re-tensioned, then thwang! A cable snapped and sacks dropped onto the rocks below.

Norman and Donald thought the only solution was physically to shoulder the sacks to the plucking area so, frustrated, Dods called for the Blondin to be abandoned and requested all hands to transport the heavy sacks to Bruinhilda's cairn where heaps of birds already lay cooling in readiness for plucking the next day.

In the lowering sun of another day, tarpaulins were thrown over the pile of birds to prevent the black-backed gulls from stabbing out the hearts of the gugas – an irresistible delicacy that could spoil a good catch.

We walked wearily back to headquarters together and sat by the cook bothy for our meal. Constellations of early stars appeared overhead as we ate porridge from our bowls in the chill of the evening air.

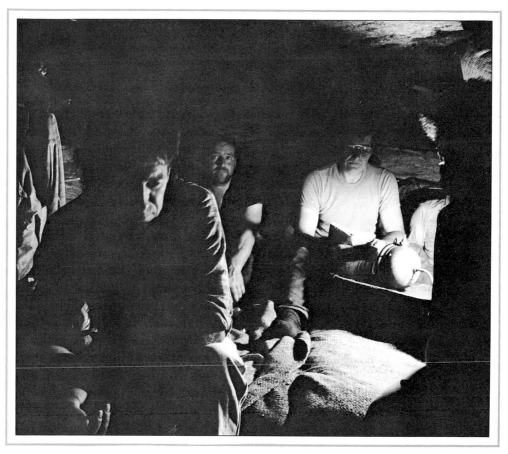

Within the gloom of the stone beehive dwellings, after each communal meal,
Murdo Campbell makes a reading from the Gaelic bible.

Murdo is a part-time weaver and a veteran guga hunter. He is a softly-spoken and powerful man who exercises a strong influence on the squad.

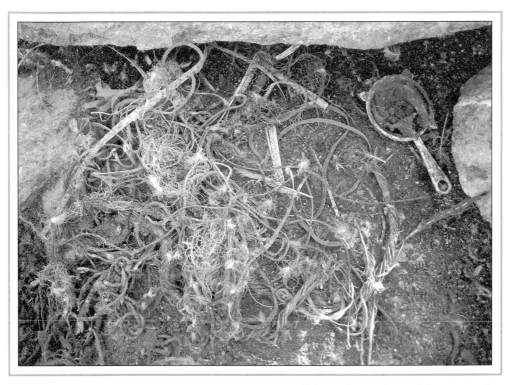

The gannet's nest is made from material gathered from the surface of the sea and from amongst the rocks of the island. More recently, trash – especially masses of plastic string from fish-netting – makes up the majority of the nesting material. Many birds become entangled in the string, injuring themselves.

Between the two main promontories are deep inlets in the cliffs called zawns. In these steep sections, other birds like kittiwakes and shags have their nests.

An unmanned, automatic lighthouse crowns the highest point of Sula Sgeir.
The gannets' largest colony is situated by the light.

Before the men move down the cliffs, the top of the rock near the lighthouse is harvested. This is a rich area for prime quality gugas.

The catching and killing of the gugas is swift and decisive. Up to 200 birds can be taken in a hunt lasting half an hour.

Only certain gugas are selected. The white downy chicks will be left to fledge and
will return to Sula Sgeir in three years' time when they are mature.

Within the restricted confines of the descent gully, Norman Macdonald acts as middle man as the gugas are handed in a human chain up the cliff.

Amidst heavy rain and deep mud, the men gather the gugas. Each man in the hunting team has a specific task: one to catch, one to kill, one to decapitate. Once the hunt is finished, everyone helps to gather the birds into piles.

The decapitated guga are handed man to man from the colony sites to the collecting areas where they are piled up before being placed in sacks.

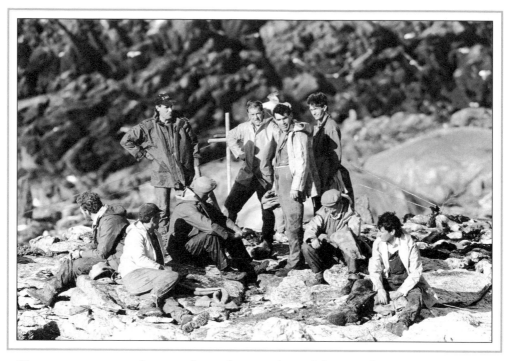

The gugas are carried across the rocks in sacks and deposited near the 'Blondins' where the plucking will take place. The men rest briefly after each strenuous excursion across the slippery rocks.

Twice a day, at 12 noon and at 5.00 in the afternoon, Calum Mackay – who is acting as cook this year – brings a kettle of hot tea to the work site. A strange picnic in this desolate place.

The men always walk together to ensure economy of rest times, and in single file so that no one needs to pass in opposite directions amongst the awkward boulders.

The hessian sacks each contain ten birds. They are hooked on to the suspended 'Blondin' wires on pulleys, and slid down above the boulder-strewn island to the collecting area called the 'factory'.

5. Sunlight and Sabbath

A warm breeze played across the island. In an eggshell-blue sky, fulmars and gannets swirled in updraughts of light air. The Sabbath was becoming a rare and beautiful day. There was no work whatsoever to be done, a strictly held tradition of Lewis people. There was, of course, nowhere to go and nothing to do but enjoy our summery rock.

Decked out in my shorts, I wandered along the bare shelving tidal slabs in search of seals. Kittiwakes crouched on tiny ledges in the vertical walls of a shadowy stack rock. One flitted out to reveal spectacular and vivid wing-bars, perfect camouflage against the sea foam. It twisted and turned and uttered shrieking cries, all wholly appropriate to its dashing lines. Young shags were sitting low in the turquoise water, their snake heads dipping under as if to look for fish; then, with the fluidity of mercury, they sprang over in an exquisite arch to disappear beneath the surface, apparently never to be seen again. I scanned the inlet in which they were fishing, each time trying to guess where they would emerge.

Along the tideline scurried groups of turnstones, feeding nervously through the thick stalks of seaweed. It was stunning to observe two colours in nature so identical, the russet tone of the small birds matching that of the wrack on which they fed.

I found a comfortable ledge on which to sit, out of the breeze and in full sunshine. I turned down my collar, closed my eyes and stretched out in blissful relaxation. The sea beat the rocks below me, sucking and swishing in the heavy weed; oyster-catchers in a distant zawn pip-pipped a sweet alarm. Beneath my palms, the crystalline rocks felt ancient and solid.

There were voices round the corner. I sat up and, in doing so, startled a huge grey seal whose flippers thrashed the water and was gone. Over the back of my rock was an area of emerald-green tidal pools, fringed with soft fronds of feathery algae. Around the largest pool sat four of the men, laughing and talking together while they bathed their feet in the clear water. On each Sabbath for centuries before, men must have used this pool for the same purpose, and have sat together in relaxed communion of a kind unknown since their childhood.

Sunday meant clean clothes and honest rest, and down here at the pool with their trousers rolled up to their knees, they whiled away the day in holiday style.

With permission from the elders, I had been allowed to bring onto the Rock with me a good friend from home and an assistant from many a photo adventure. Stuart Dale is a short, rough and to-the-point kind of person; industrious and easy going, he was an ideal companion on the bleak island.

We walked together out onto a section of the island rarely visited except on Sundays. It was a curious promontory, almost severed from its mother island and rising in a whaleback of clean, dry rock. For some reason, few birds nested up there save for a dozen or so gulls' nests that crowned the haughty summit. I suspect winter storms blasted the place so severely that all the vestiges of shelter and protection for a colony to form simply didn't exist. These slabs of rock were so open to winds from all quarters that only the skin of sulphur lichens survived. On the summit, we found masses of broken seashells, bleached crabs and small bones. I thought it might be a spot where the black-backs dropped their food from a considerable height in order to break it up, enabling them to devour the softer parts.

The view of Sula Sgeir from here was quite the best on the island. Below us, the creek into which we had sailed what now seemed weeks ago glistened in the afternoon haze. Hidden from view were the vast gannet colonies of the Lighthouse and Chapel Promontories, and they were revealed only by the clouds of birds on the wing and the swirling vortices of fishing flocks offshore. Our bothies sited on the only green sward on the side of the col had thin twirls of smoke rising from their domes. Two or three of the men were sitting outside drinking tea.

This gave us ideas of our own and we hurried back to camp, taking care at the junction of the promontories since a dangerous stride is required to cross a deep chasm that reached down to a dark plunging sea. The kettle was not quite drained so we re-heated the dregs and added some fresh bags. I ducked too quickly into my bothy and zapped my head on the entrance's low lintel and ended up sitting semi-dazed on my bench, my mug of tea getting cold.

The gloom inside the bothy was frightful on such a fine day so we rugged up in jackets and over-trousers and sat out on the cliffs until darkness fell.

The sky of Sula Sgeir is full of birds on the wing. Newly-fledged fulmars coast in the eddies above the cliffs.

The sheltered creek of Geodh à Phuill Bhàin in the shimmering light of a
fine summer's morning.

Young shags fishing close to the rocks in the surging tide.

Sunday is a day of rest when no work is done. Kenny Murray and Dods Macfarlane, on the left, bathe their feet in a tidal rockpool. Opposite is Carrots Norman, the youngest of the team, and Donald Macfarlane, Dods's brother. This same washing place has been used for decades.

Left: In 1983, Murdo Macfarlane, the father of Dods and Donald, left a message hidden inside a bottle in a cairn on Sula Sgeir. The message described how appalling the weather had been that year and how wet everyone had become – so wet for Murdo that he had hardly ever been warm and so vowed never to return to the rock. Murdo had been out on the hunt for well over thirty years before his decision and had made the dangerous passage many times in an open boat.

The men remain inside the bothies for most of the day on the Sabbath. They chat and relax, occasionally emerging to walk over the rocks to wash in the pools. Inside, the peat fires are kept burning all day; often clothes are washed and left out to dry.

Calum Mackay cooks all our meals. He is an experienced veteran of twenty-two visits to the rock. As well as cooking, he lends his hand to the key work of processing the birds.

6. Down on the Rocks

At six thirty the next morning, we all gathered at Bruinhilda's cairn to pluck the birds that were now nicely dried off by the summery breeze that the Sabbath had brought. The rocks by the cairn formed a natural turret that was exposed to the wind but for some reason was devoid of nesting fulmars. Perhaps they don't nest on sacred ground.

Dods demonstrated his method of plucking: first, he laid the bird between his knees and plucked the neck, leaving a narrow collar of feathers; then he snatched fistfuls of feathers from the breast area as far down as the tail, and ripped off the new primaries from the upper wing, pinching off the leading edge quills. Then he turned the bird over and plucked the back and legs until only pure white feathery down remained. It was a lot easier said than done. Though Dods could pluck a guga in two or three minutes, I found my fingers skidding off the muddy feathers and soon grew so tired I could hardly pinch at all, constantly having to rest and shake out my hands. In exasperation, I sometimes pressed too hard, causing the stinking contents of the bird's crop to ooze out of the neck and on to my lap.

The white birds in the pile were that much younger and had more down amongst the feathers. Bobby tipped me off that they were easier to pluck and I took his advice although embarrassed should the others spot me choosing an easy bird. Each hour, Dods called for a tally of plucked birds. It soon became quite competitive and read: Dods 27, Murdo 25, Kenny 21, Norman Macdonald – who was in the squad for the first time – 15. His score was accompanied by unfair peals of laughter. Then it was my turn.

'Nine,' I called out quite proudly.

'Well done, John,' said Kenny. 'You only need to triple that rate and you can come to Sula Sgeir again.' More laughter.

By now, the air was filled with feathers blowing about like snow. Finlay and Donald were sitting submerged in a sea of down, like chicks in an eagle's giant eyrie. There was feather and down in our hair, up our noses and in our ears. There was some cursing, a lot of spitting but always a grim determination to keep up the pace. The work was hard but rewarding and even before breakfast the daily quota was complete and ready for the next phase.

As we left our perch and ambled down for breakfast, we saw my assistant Stu emerge from his bothy. He had been sleeping in for a couple of hours and only appeared now for breakfast. Immediately Dods was at him. 'Ooh, long lie the day, Stu boy, long lie the day?' he said in a voice loud enough for everyone to hear. A gentle gibe, but one a Lewisian rarely hears. Stu, being Manchester born and bred, looked up slowly and said laconically, 'Ay, Dods, I reckon it is,' and went back to rolling papers round his pinch of tobacco and squinting into the bright morning light.

Outside the cooking bothy were several buckets of murky water for hand-washing before meals. This was often residual water from the previous year. We queued up to scrub our hands and wrists with brushes that would have graced our doorsteps back home. We shook our hands dry and ducked inside the dark tunnel to squeeze into a shoulder's-width space on the ledges inside.

Calum had been preparing breakfast for about an hour, the kettle was hanging on a hook above the peats and simmering nicely. Laid across the top of the peat keg was a wire grid onto which we put thick slices of bread to make smoky slices of toast. The plates had been warming; we each took one and the box of odd cutlery was passed round. Finlay raked amongst it for his favourite irons. Finlay was a very quiet man, he talked little and usually only when spoken to, but he was nonetheless friendly and easy company out on the rock. Sitting on the end of his bench, he asked me why I had wanted to come here. 'For the breakfasts,' I joked.

Calum waited until we were all settled and balanced with plates and cutlery on our knees before handing round the grill tray. In neat stacks, floating in a millimetre of oil, were twelve breakfasts of black pudding, bacon, eggs and fried bread. 'Carrots' Norman – the youngest, and one of the hardest working of the clan – had proudly produced white puddings for us all from his butcher's business back on Lewis. Once in the grill tray, the puddings fell apart and revealed chunks of cold suet.

Dods held up some on his fork and in a tirade of Gaelic banter proclaimed the puddings as inedible. This precipitated some more gentle haranguing and ended with Carrots' final words: 'Aaargh, take it or leave it, man.' By the end of breakfast, all the food was eaten, every rind and every crust and, quite sated, we crawled out into daylight to continue our morning's work.

Up at the Blondin line, Donald Macfarlane, who is Dods's brother, and Carrots were struggling to secure the wooden stanchions that helped to give tension to the wire cables but they were not stable enough to allow further torque to be transferred on to the wires. With a strong hand from the others, and a lot of shouting in the gathering wind, the task of sending down the sacks to the 'factory' area finally began.

Ten plucked birds were put in every sack, and on a signal it was released to slide 150 metres down to the more sheltered col above the landing creek where the next stage of the operation took place. The returning empty sack, joined by pulleys and strings, swished upwards to be refilled until the pile at the plucking site was cleared. As the heavy sack neared the bottom, Dods controlled its speed by frictioning a bird's wing over the cable and string. Sometimes a sack would dangle lifelessly out in space and would need hauling in with the strings. The lines kept sagging, the cable tensions were wrong and the system halted.

Frustration developed into anger and at the height of everyone's misery, a string broke and one sack accelerated down the cableway towards Murdo, its velocity increasing alarmingly. Murdo dived to one side as the entire sackful of birds crashed through the stanchions, smashing the stays and snapping yet another cable. Dods vowed to rethink the system for next year. To catch up the lost time, we all spent an hour shouldering loads down through the sea spinach.

As we tramped by, the fulmar chicks automatically vomited vile-smelling stomach oil but finally they were spent and sat blinking in apparent bewilderment at the passage of so many feet.

The gannet, *Sula bassana*, only comes to rocky islets to breed. The collective sound of hundreds of thousands of gannets on Sula Sgeir is deafening.

The daunting approach to Sula Sgeir.

The island's bleak promontories are crowded with gannets.

To assist transference of equipment and eventually the guga harvest, a crude
wooden chute is built down the broken rock-face from the top of the island.

The men of Ness probe deeply into the steepest cliffs of the Chapel Promontory.
They risk wet and slippery rocks and high winds during each hunt.

The selection of each bird is a vital part of the guga harvest.

Only the darker-phase birds are taken.

Three phases of the process: singeing, de-winging and splitting, and sending down the chute to be transferred to the trawler.

The exact positioning within the wheel formation on the pickling stack is crucial.

At Port of Ness, the gugas are apportioned evenly, and made ready for sale.

Sula Sgeir, the gannet rock.

If the gugas are soaking wet from hours of incessant rain, they must be laid out on
the rocks and dried in the wind before they can be plucked.

All the gugas have to be plucked. This is done away on the island's highest rocks, out on the open slabs near Bruinhilda's cairn. It is a very communal job but there is little talking since the work is hard and competitive.

These plucking scenes remind me how ancient this tradition is, sitting out on the windy rocks under the Atlantic sky, snatching at the gugas' feathers. There has been little change in this practice over the centuries.

Kenny sits with his back to the wind. In the chilly early morning sea-mist, the gugas are damp and difficult to pluck.

In the lee shelter of Bruinhilda's cairn, Norman Macdonald – on his first visit to the island – learns that plucking is a mixture of technique and brute strength.

Dods keeps a careful note of the numbers of birds plucked, principally to keep to the annual quota accorded by the Nature Conservancy Council's agreement.

Dods himself plucks up to thirty-five birds an hour. There is no escape from the downy feathers which blow into the eyes, nose, ears and hair.

Waiting for the bible reading after breakfast. From the left: Dods Macfarlane,
Murdo Campbell, Kenny Murray, Finlay Morrison and Angus Murdo Gunn.

The scene inside the beehive dwelling might have been from a century ago; instead, it is the summer of 1991. Toast is made on the wire grill over the peats. Dods is shown outlining the day's work; next to him is Kenny, then Stuart Dale my assistant, Donald Macfarlane and Bobby Morrison.

Dods holds open a hessian sack as Carrots fills it with ten plucked gugas. These will be hooked on to the Blondin wires and sent down to the factory area.

Once the sack is full, it is sent by gravity down the Blondin wires to a lower section on the rocks.

Murdo receives the sacks at the bottom, whilst Norman carries the birds a few yards
to the factory area for the next stage.

Murdo releases the neck of the sack to offload the gugas; then he signals for the empty sack to be pulled back up the line by the next descending sack.

When the Blondin cables snap, the heavy sacks have to be man-handled several hundred yards across the boulder-strewn rocks to the factory area.

7. Walking the Yardarm

*L*eaning on the wind by the lighthouse, I strained my eyes onto the rocks below to try to spot which route the two hunting parties had taken. From here, it seemed impossible for anyone to descend the massive cliff at this point. Below the light, it was quite vertical for thirty metres. Then a platform of pure white rock extended to the south-west for 100 metres; raised high above the sea, it was the yardarm of the island. It was at the farthest point from the bothies and since we intended staying out here the whole day, Stu had brought all the cameras and film, also a safety rope, harnesses and windproofs. We were heavily burdened and it was little wonder that the party quickly disappeared and left us to find our own way. They had a long and busy day ahead in order to harvest this most spectacular platform that they called the Altar Rocks, and then to bring the quarry back across the island.

The Altar Rocks were quite unlike any other part of Sula Sgeir. Dried guano was so thick here it had smoothed out all the crevices and textures of the rock and with constant wind-blasting and salt spray had become dry and shiny like white marble. From high above, we had an incredible view.

The men suddenly appeared from the shadow of the cliffs below and began their work. The adult birds took to the air with a clamour and hung above us on the airstream in vast numbers. I remembered Dods's father, back on Lewis, had remarked to me that at Altar Rocks the gannets were so numerous they were 'like the arrows of the Greeks'.

The two teams moved in a pincer movement, clearing the edges and then sweeping across the flat top of the rock. There seemed to be no undue alarm from the colony down there. It was as though we were watching in slow motion. Behind the wave of hunters, there was stillness: ahead, a rich harvest. The pincer closed at the furthest promontory of white rock. Pools of scarlet interspaced the small heaps of birds. The chicks which were not taken shuffled back to their nests while the men stopped for a while under the cliff for a cigarette. The adult gannets remained above, hanging in the air like a mobile over a baby's cradle.

Abandoning our ropes because of the wind, Stu and I scrambled precariously down a steep gully on the east side of the lighthouse. A vertical step led us into a deep bay of rock, and then a narrow gangway led out onto the open flat rocks. Here we found the men discussing how to ascend the vertiginous walls of the Altar in view of the wind's strength. Bobby pulled out a fraying plastic rope and Stu buried his head. Being extremely safety conscious, the thought of such rock antics obviously appalled him.

I followed Bobby and Norman to the far point of the promontory; they were going to act as the cliff-top support team to Dods and Kenny working below. The rocks were slippery and awkward here; cakes of guano under my boots and steady high winds unnerved me for a time. I could see Stu didn't like it either.

Kenny slid over the edge of the rock towards the sea, stopped and reached back to receive the catching pole from Dods. I leaned over as far as I dared to see them. The wind was offshore on this side, so I scrambled down some steep ledges to share a niche with three downy gugas in a hollow sheltered from the full force of the wind. Kenny and Dods were shouting below: they had reached an impasse and needed a safety rope from Bobby. He was above me now, uncoiling the plastic rope. Norman took up the spare coils and wedged himself in a crevice while Bobby leaned out dangerously over a yawning drop to cast an accurate line for the two below. The gap in the ledge system that Dods had to cross was wet and smooth. The sea below sucked up and down the wall like a breathing creature. They said some words together and smiled, then Dods reached out over the gap. In all the decades of time that this harvest has been taken, there has never been an accident on the cliffs.

Dods called up for some tension on the rope. Bobby leaned forward at a horrific angle – all I could think of was three men catapulting off the cliff. Stu couldn't take any more and retired from the action, returning to the slabby bay below the lighthouse. The rope went slack, Norman relaxed in his crevice and Kenny decided not to follow Dods any further. Dods worked alone for half an hour, collecting perhaps only a score of birds. This section of cliff was so precipitous that Bobby pulled the birds fixed on the rope in bundles of four at a time. No easy task since each one weighed about nine pounds. I clambered back up the windy ledges, being careful not to appear full face on a bird ledge since Carrots had been pecked in the eye only days before.

Bobby was sitting resting with a heap of birds round his feet. 'What do you think, John? You've seen it now,' he said, shouting through the wind and drawing on a cigarette. He then went on to tell me that coming to Sula Sgeir each year was for him the best holiday he could imagine. Of all the lads in the team this year, Bobby was the biggest. A perfect anchor man and a voracious worker. He was born in a small house on top of the cliffs within sight of the open boats in Skigersta harbour.

Calum's kettle miraculously appeared mid-afternoon and although tepid was most welcome. It was lowered down the cliff on a rope to our worksite in the rock bay. Stu was shivering: he had been here most of the day in the shadows, and was now quite bemused since the gugas had been gathered up and were heaped around him knee-deep. Kenny mentioned Joan of Arc and we all broke out laughing, Stu included.

Working late in the far reaches of the island meant a flurry of activity before dinner. The only way to get the bird pile to the lighthouse was by a chain gang handing the birds one by one up the cliff. We spread out, bridging across corners, pinned in the backs of gullies, balanced on rocky boulders, and we bodily lifted every bird man to man until the site was clear. We were a quiet and tired group at dinner that night, especially when Dods announced the work was not quite over. Some of the previous day's guga catch had not been plucked. He planned to fire up the tilly lamp and work until midnight.

In the strange atmosphere of the stillness of night, we plucked birds for two hours. Only the yellow glow from our lamp illuminated the ghostly task and once more I was chilled by the proximity of ancients who had sat here once before beneath oil lamps, snatching at the feathers of birds, and honouring the fathers of time.

The white guano-covered rocks at the south end of the island, below the lighthouse, are densely crowded with gannets. This area is called the Altar Rocks. The hunters work quickly across the top before descending the steep 200 ft high cliffs on either side.

After the gugas are killed, Finlay gathers up the birds into small heaps, ready to be collected.

Norman coils a safety rope ready for future use, while Donald collects the birds into heaps before they are put into sacks.

Carrots collects up equipment used on the Altar Rocks, the catching pole, a stout stick and a knife.

A brief rest during the hunt. The men sit on the Altar Rocks before carrying the gugas up the steep cliffs, one by one.

Carrots looks across the heaps of gugas, making an approximate count before they are taken up the cliffs.

To the east, a very steep gully leads into the lower colonies of birds. The men arrange themselves precariously in the groove, ready to pass the gugas up the cliff.

On the south-west side of the promontory rocks, the men descend to the lower ledges with catching poles.

Ropes are often required on dangerous sections of the cliff. Two men are usually stationed above those working below to act as safety support. In this picture, Norman, on the left, makes himself reasonably secure by standing firmly in a crevice; Bobby monitors the operation from the edge of the cliff.

When required, a rope is cast down to those working below – either as safety support or for hauling bundles of birds up the steep cliffs.

Bobby makes the perfect anchor man, supporting Dods and Kenny working below
on wet, holdless rocks.

When the cliffs are too steep for passing the birds up by hand, they are hauled up in bundles of four. This is some burden as each bird weighs up to 9 lbs.

Murdo wedges himself in the steep descent gully to control the harvest being
passed up the cliff.

Dods makes his way across a dangerous section of rocks, safeguarded by a rope from above. Kenny stays further back.

The day's work is not quite over for Norman. In order to keep to schedule, birds are plucked by the light of a tilly lamp until midnight.

8. Fire to the Foundry

*L*ighting peats was not easy, most were wet from days of incessant rain and out there on a prominence high about the creek, each day and in all weathers, the fires were lit to singe the down from the plucked gugas. Two turrets of stone were built, a metre square like the tops of small chimneys. A hearth was prepared on a base of loose stone onto which the peats were carefully placed. A strong draught or, better, a wind was needed to fan the glow to flames. The direction of the wind was critical so, through the decades, the hearths have remained in the same positions, raised up in order to receive the westerly gale.

Glowing peats from the bothies were carried across the rocks with iron tongs as if from the foundry of a Norse myth, and introduced into the hearths. Gizzards from another process were laid carefully banked up on the windward side of the peats, for when the flames licked the gizzards, the fats melted into the peats, creating a roaring furnace of blazing oils. As soon as the fire was leaping from the mouth of the structure, a bird was presented to the flames.

Kenny snapped a guga's wing joints with a deft crack across his waist and then, by holding its wings as a handle, he dipped the bird into the flames, flicking it about, swivelling it back and forth. The feathery down dissolved instantly to fine black ash; the webbed feet curled to a crisp. The singeing process was critical to the exact flavour of the bird – too much and the skin would burn, too little and the quills could spoil the texture. Kenny and Angus took on the heavy duties of singeing this year. Every bird had to pass through the flames. The labour of feeding the fires and flaming the birds soon led to an aching back and tender fingers. Calum stepped into help, taking time off from his kitchen duties. He could take on most tasks since he had been part of the hunt for twenty-two years.

The 'factory' was now in full process. Norman brought plucked birds to the fires, and took singed birds to the finishing area. The ash was scrubbed off with a brush by Carrots who wore protective goggles in case any of the tiny, fine quill stubs entered his eyes. He handed the clean birds on to Finlay and Bobby who sat and laboriously checked the quality control with blow torches.

Sitting nearby, and within arms' reach, Donald sat astride a chopping block and struck off the wings with a hand axe. He gave the bird a final brushing down and then laid it at his side for splitting. To complete the 'factory' circle, a long heavy beam was balanced on two crates or barrels. Facing each other astride the beam, Murdo and Dods performed the vital process of separation. With razor-sharp knives, each guga was split from end to end, and the tail removed. Three exacting cuts outside the rib cage were made next and then, with fingers plunged between flesh and bone, the neck, entire rib cage and entrails were drawn from the carcase in one strong pull and cast in a heap for readiness for laying onto the singeing fires. Four neat cuts were then made behind each nub of flesh to create pockets that would retain the pickling salt. The flaccid skin and meat were carefully laid out on tarpaulins to await the salting process. The smell, especially after a few days of the singeing process, the separating and the salting can, at best, be said to be astringent.

The splitting beam had seen many seasons on Sula Sgeir and each year the splitter carved his dated name on it; after the men left the island, it lay beside one of the beehive bothies to weather out the winter storms, a redundant totem to be exorcised each year by a new harvester.

The ground on which the pickling gugas lay was prepared carefully. All sharp stones were removed and replaced by flat slabs – this therefore was the only absolutely flat ground on Sula Sgeir. This was essential to prevent the vital pickle from leaking out; an inadequately salted guga would ruin the quality of the harvest. Once again, it was Kenny and Dods who prepared this key stage and first laid out a plastic sheet across the rock. The first gugas were laid down in a wheel formation, with feet turned to the centre, the outside flap of skin being folded over to prevent leakage. The second row would overlap and lie closer to the centre and so on, until the first entire layer was formed. A second, third and fourth layer were added quickly. The exact position and angle of every single bird was fussed over and checked for level. The pile began to rise. As the days passed, it rose spectacularly – a symbolic wheel of meat.

Every day, when the nightly tarpaulin was removed from the stack, there were pools of pickling fluids in amongst the flesh. Each day, these were tasted for quality. There is no process in the story of the guga more carefully monitored than this one: it was the key to the vintage.

During the afternoon of our second Sabbath on the island, Calum was busy preparing a feast, perhaps the most traditional gourmet meal I may ever eat, and out there in the Atlantic, squatting in a stone bothy, it was the perfect place to enjoy it. On the menu that night was guga.

Around mid-afternoon, I left the others relaxing by the rock pools and went to help Calum, and to learn how to cook the 'beast'. For twelve people, only three birds were needed, and I was assured that this would be quite enough. First, we washed the filleted birds thoroughly, winkling out all the salt. Already I could see this was going to be a greasy affair. Each bird was cut into four portions, each one scraped scrupulously clean with a small sharp knife.

Cooking was simple: boiled for one hour, with a water-change after thirty minutes. It was traditional to eat guga only with boiled potatoes.

That same evening at eight o'clock, in gathering darkness, we all arrived, especially cleaned up for the feast. The huge pot was standing on the peats with the gugas bubbling and frothing in the brown water. Potatoes were handed around on the plates, dry and steamy. Then portions of the 'beast' were lifted from the pot and distributed amongst the twelve. Some of us had breast meat and extra skin, some just skin and claws and a little meat, but each portion was even in size. It came as no surprise to find that no cutlery was to be used, but we were to pull the meat apart with our fingers. I was advised on how to proceed.

'Now, John, watch,' demonstrated Kenny. 'A mouthful of skin and a mouthful of potato, all in one, down it goes. Very good, John, ay?'

I tried it and sure enough this was a special meal. They all watched my face; I kept steady. 'Mmm, amazing. Very good,' I concurred. The taste was quite extraordinary. It had the texture of good steak and the taste of kipper. It had a definite sense of being from the sea. It was neither fish nor fowl, but somewhere in between.

At my side, I noticed Donald nibbling the skin from between the claws. 'The best bit, John, try it.'

We slid our fingers into the hot grease among the bones and tore off strips of tasty skin which was not unlike good Lancashire tripe. Everyone was fairly quiet, concentrating on picking out all the good meat. And, no doubt, they were reflecting with some reverence the act which they performed each year to honour this ancient tradition and to think quietly of their fathers who had sat in this same bothy and had enjoyed the guga supper before them. I sat in my place on the cramped bench and thought of the only man to have died on Sula Sgeir, a man who, many years ago, had choked on a guga bone that had lodged in his throat.

On the earth floor, by the hot barrel of glowing peats, was a plastic food box. Dods invited me to look inside and I carefully opened the lid. Sitting in the corner was a tiny ball of dark grey fluff with an unmistakable beak and large obsidian eyes blinking at the sudden light; it was a storm petrel chick. It had tumbled from its nest within the bothy walls, and Dods was looking after it until its parents returned in the night. Cupped in his strong hands, the tiny bird was safe for now. It was as we were finishing our tea that we heard the plaintive twirling whistle of an adult 'stormy'. From out of the dark night fluttered the parent bird; she flew through our tunnel entrance and flopped on the floor at our feet, shuffled onto a box and disappeared into a crevice in the cold stone walls. Dods gently posted the downy chick after her. It was not incongruous but a measure of the range of spirit these men possessed, fortitude, resilience and a gift of grace.

The singeing process is swift and critical; the down feathers can only be lightly burned or the taste will be impaired. Kenny works for hours at the fire.

Often Kenny and Calum work together. The gizzards are laid on the windward side of the hearth to allow the melted fat to drip into the peats.

On a high prominence above the landing creek, the two ancient hearths are exposed to strong winds from the south and west. It is here that for centuries the singeing fires have been sited, like a scene from a Norse myth.

The newly singed gugas are brushed clean by Carrots (wearing goggles), de-winged by Donald, and then split by Dods and Murdo astride the beam.

A blowtorch is used to remove the remaining quills from the bird. Bobby erected a makeshift wind-shelter to stabilise the gas jet.

Once plucked, the guga goes through the entire 'factory' process immediately or it may spoil. Astride the beam, Dods and Murdo are splitting the birds in readiness for salting and stacking. The gizzards removed at this stage are returned to the singeing fire to boost the fiery peats.

A fistful of salt is pushed into each of four pockets of meat, then cast all over the guga. The salted carcase is next taken to be put on the pickling stack.

The pickling stack is a surprising, intriguing and somewhat intimidating sight as it grows; it is constructed like a broch, a symbol of power.

The gugas on the outside of the pile have their skin turned inwards so the vital preserving pickles do not leak out. The development and retention of the pickle is the key to the quality and taste of the bird. The guga stack is situated near the chute to ease departure when the time arrives.

The fulmar petrel is the invasive bird present on Sula Sgeir. Eventually, it will overcrowd the gannet colonies. Walking across the island is made most unpleasant by the chicks' natural habit of reflex-vomiting at any passer-by. Once fledged, however, the fulmar is an object of great beauty, a supreme flyer of ocean winds.

To prepare the guga to eat, Calum scrapes the outside skin clean with a sharp knife.
A quarter of a bird is ample for each person.

Three gugas are in the pot, boiling and ready to be served in an hour's time. The water is changed after half an hour so excess grease can be poured off.

Traditionally, the guga is eaten with boiled potatoes, and no cutlery is used. The bird tastes like something between a steak and a kipper.

From the left, Norman, Murdo and Finlay share one beehive 'house'. There is great camaradarie amongst the men on Sula Sgeir.

9. Departure ————————————————

*T*he weather men were forecasting a south-easterly five to six. This was bad news for it is impossible to land on Sula Sgeir with a blow from that quarter. Only finishing duties were needed now and a restlessness came over the team. To leave Sula Sgeir with the harvest complete and to return home safely to Port of Ness has long been the subject of epic sea stories. I didn't want to depart from this place and be part of such history, nor did I relish the prospect of five extra days here when food and especially water was running low. Even that morning, I had delivered a loaf of bread up to the cook bothy that contained at least thirty earwigs.

On the side of the col behind the largest beehive dwelling was a circular ruin, the roof of which had long since tumbled in. Years ago it was used as an isolation house for one unfortunate hunter who had brought scarlet fever with him to the island. Since then, it has never been inhabited. It was 1 p.m. and Dods was crouching within its walls out of the wind, tuning in his CB radio to speak to Stornoway in the hope of arranging an accurate time schedule for leaving the Rock. Perhaps the wind would swing back to the west and what then? Would Dods leave on a morning tide? We would not decommission the bothies until the returning boat was in sight and, at this point, we still had one hundred birds in the 'factory' line.

Kenny was the first to ask Dods if there was any news. He was anxious to know in case there would be time for him to join the Ness soccer-team's excursion to Inverness the following weekend; this was a team with an awesome reputation in the Highlands & Islands amateur league. There was much talk of life at home during that day. Before, only the Rock and the hard work involved were discussed. I thought of their lives at home, of their family and of their parents, all anxious to hear news of their arrival back on the mainland and how, each year, the safe return of these men represents a cohesion in the community's life and a celebration of rich harvest.

The following day was brightening to hot sun. I abandoned the factory area and walked up through the colonies of gannets to enjoy the clearing mist out on the cliffs. Parent birds were flying into the nests, disgorging fish and feeding hungry chicks. The young fulmars, stronger now in the turbulent eddies, wheeled and floated in the dazzling light. Some way offshore, I could see North Rona, the green island fourteen miles to the east, a place of great mystery and romance, and intrinsically linked with the history of sea journeys to Sula Sgeir.

Bobby hailed me from Bruinhilda's cairn and gestured out to sea. Sure enough, in the far distance to the south and barely visible in the silver sea, a tiny dot was approaching. I ran excitedly down to the chute where all the men had gathered. Around the corner of the island came the trawler, the engine was cut and she rolled into the creek on the swell. Not since my days in Greenland and Antarctica had I felt that precious mixture of relief and joy, tinged with a sadness that comes at the end of a supreme adventure.

Kenny and Dods were soon in the rubber dinghy, ferrying mooring lines to the cliff. The covers of netting and sheeting were unrolled off the bothy roofs, all the cooking pots and pans which had been neatly made ready were going in turn down to the rocks. Carrots placed a mattress at the base of the chute, for soon the pile of gugas would be unstacked and the birds slid down to sea level. Everyone was working hard and efficiently. Murdo ominously placed a last stone onto his cairn. All domestic luggage waited at the top of the chute, ready for lowering. Boxes and bags were shoved down the chute and stacked on ledges below. Down came the car battery and empty water barrels restrained on a rope. The tilly lamp was carried separately down the cliff.

We gathered for a quick brew of tea at the top of the rocky stairway. Everything was now ready for the final phase – the gugas' descent to the waterline, transfer into the punt, and departure out to the waiting trawler. Our schedule of four hours for this whole operation depended on our arriving in Ness on an upcoming deepwater tide. We had to work quickly.

Up at the guga pile, Donald and Norman loosened the top layer of birds and began to send them, one by one, down the chute. Although it was a slow business at first, the wooden planks of the chute were soon glistening in pickle and grease and each bird slid easily down onto an untidy heap on the mattress at the bottom. Calum was there to throw them into the punt from where they were ferried to the hold of the trawler. The punt sat very low in the water by the time each load was ready for the off. If the swell had been any higher, it would have been a very precarious passage. We motored slowly across the black water. Two young lads were up on deck to cast the gugas into the hold. Dods was also on board, making radio contact with Ness, and the skipper already had a guga boiling in the galley.

I stood on deck and gazed at the Chapel Promontory, its bristling cairns and finger stones silhouetting a calvary on the black crown of Sula Sgeir. Gannets and fulmars soared silently through the cols and pinnacles. I heard the hiss of air across their wings and was lost in thought for a moment. Then I gathered myself for the return home.

Dods Macfarlane made a daily radio call to the Isle of Lewis to confirm the safety of everyone on the rock. Here he is speaking to the trawler about its return.

Once the returning trawler is sighted, the tarpaulins and netting are taken off the
beehive dwellings, and stored inside for another year.

Each man has a personal cairn of stones; Murdo Campbell has placed another stone on his cairn for good luck, and makes ready to leave the island for another year.

All the equipment, apart from the dismantled chute and the roof coverings, return with the men. Finlay helps gear slide smoothly down the chute.

On the given word, the tarps over the guga piles are removed and the great stacks
dismantled. Norman and Donald work for an hour at this task.

The boat can only remain in the creek for a few hours, so work is intense. The discarded wings will blow away in the autumn gales, leaving no trace.

After the gear and personal belongings are down the chute, the gugas are slid down. Murdo casts them on the rocks near to the punt.

On top of the guga load in the punt, other supplies are taken out to the waiting trawler. The men work like well-oiled clockwork.

Calum casts the gugas from the foot of the chute into the punt. The tide swell, rising and falling against the rocks, indicates that time is running out.

Kenny is in charge of transferring each load to the trawler. The makeshift radio
aerial is dismantled for another year.

The gugas are thrown from the punt on to the deck of the trawler, and then into the hold. The schedule of work to be done before departure is nearly finished.

Sula Sgeir will remain without habitation until the men return next year. The chicks will fledge and leave the rock before the autumn gales and pounding winter seas.

10. Released but not Forgotten ─────────

Calum released the final mooring lines and slithered down the thick
seaweed. With a strong push-off, he hopped into the rubber dinghy and
motored across to the trawler. We were now all on board and all out on deck,
settling into corners and doorways and preparing, each in his own way, to face
the huge seas out beyond the shelter of the creek. I wondered if it was a good
idea to eat the guga which was being handed round as token morsels.

The boat lurched as the swell increased in the mouth of Geodha à Phuill
Bhàin. The diesel fired, and we swung out into the southerly blow. Only four
hundred metres off the Rock, the waves became mountainous. Sula Sgeir
dipped behind castles of water as we plunged in a roller-coaster of deep
troughs and high ridges. I dug my fingers into the heap of fish-netting under
the stern rail, and noticed that everyone was holding on tightly. Murdo was
wedged across a doorway, Donald and Bobby leaned back to back against the
winching block.

The departing view of our island home was spectacular. We strained our
eyes upon her until she was swallowed by the sea. Sunlight danced in the
wavecrests and the great grey bulk of Sula Sgeir smoked with ten thousand
gannets pouring from its crest like a flurry of snow.

Ahead of us the sky was lowering. The island had dropped over the horizon
and had gone. Only the thrashing sea remained and the livid light on the
darkening water. Petrels glided effortlessly through the troughs, a dolphin slid
down a grey wave, and blazing silver light burst from the black horizon,
shooting yellow rays into the heavens. Curtains of rain once more swept the
sea and a languid rainbow struggled for life. Most of the men went below to
rest; only Finlay and Bobby remained on deck to watch the sea and to release
Sula Sgeir gently astern for another year.

About an hour and a half from port, everyone returned to deck and Calum
appeared with coffee all round, and then leaned on a mast stay, intent on
looking for the lighthouse on the Butt of Lewis where he is the part-time
keeper. We were within an hour of Port of Ness when the first flash was
sighted. For the fishermen among the group, the sight of the Lewis light is a
call for home, a moment of warmth to guide them into the northern Minch.

We sailed close in, past familiar skerries and the black tidal rocks of the Lewis coast and its rounded cliffs; then there was the first sight of Ness, speckled with the lights of home hearths. With binoculars, Dods peered at the quay through the darkness; he had to decide whether to anchor out in the bay until morning, or come alongside and risk a night-time unloading. The closer we came to the harbour, so details of the houses came into view, and closer still I realised the quay was thronged with people.

We made a last turn into the harbour entrance and turned on the deck floodlights. At least three hundred people surged to the very edge of the quay: some peered into the depths of the boat, trying to spot loved ones, some just waved, and all welcomed us home. For a few minutes, it was bustling mayhem. Then the men from off Sula Sgeir climbed ashore to greet their families and friends. Elderly fathers took up their positions on the edge of the quay, hoping there might be a chance to help. I scrambled up a wet iron ladder and was offered sandwiches and tea from Kenny's wife, Tina; it was a gesture I will never forget, thrust as I was into the arms of a community at the high point of their most private celebration. A row of young lads sat on the high wall above the crowds, wistfully looking on and perhaps wondering if they would ever venture to the Gannet Rock. There were babies in arms, oblivious to the laughter and chatter, and silent figures looking on from the shadows. The whole world seemed to be present to greet us back from the ocean, to welcome their heroes with lighted lamps.

A large space was formed in the throng and the first basket of shining gugas was winched from the hold. Angus Murdo's father, Donald, reached for the first basket and, helped by willing hands, cast the first heap on to the quay. The crowds shuffled back an extra step as the frightful oily smell pervaded the air. Basket after basketload was emptied onto the harbour. It was midnight and Dods decided not to sell the 'beasts' until the morning so a huge tarpaulin was thrown over them, and a guard set to watch. Everyone drifted away and the men off Sula Sgeir slipped home for their first bath for a fortnight.

By seven the next morning, the skylarks were already high over the old osier beds beyond the village, and the queue for the sales of gugas wound its way from the harbour wall to the road head. Dods and his men were busy sharing the quota evenly amongst themselves. One man looked away, out to sea, while another man pointed to a specific pile and asked the first for a name. It is through sharing, not greed, that the communities of north Lewis have survived the changing fortunes of twentieth-century life.

Most islanders order their gugas directly from one of the men who had been on the Rock and would receive the birds by special delivery direct to their homes. That day's sale was only for those who wished to buy off the quay and so numbers were limited. Supply has never met the demand for the birds. The queue on the harbour was directed through a narrow neck of parked cars and trucks. Each buyer brought a polythene bag, paid £10 for a pair of gugas, and then carried them away. There was great orderliness during the sale as folk quietly received their birds and made way for the next customer.

Whilst the men off the island might have a bird every two or three weeks throughout the winter months to share with their families or friends, most islanders would keep their pair of gugas salted or frozen until there was a special celebration or family gathering. The gugas are not so much a legacy as the heartbeat of the community.

Kenny's young children slipped and slid in the guga grease, playing around the allotted piles. At the other end of the quay, the men I had lived with for two long weeks chatted to their fathers and others who had been on the island in their time; they would have talked about this year's harvest and compared stories with the older men. There were decades of experience on the quayside that morning, re-enacting a tradition which has remained in place for some five hundred years. There were no echoes from the past now, for the six villages of Ness thrive as a modern Hebridean community. The guga hunt is perhaps a metaphor or a mystery that lies hidden only in the lives of those who go to Sula Sgeir as a symbol of thanksgiving for the bounty of the sea.

By nine o'clock, every vehicle had left the harbour, every item of equipment carried away. Only an oily sheet remained suspended over the harbour wall to be cleaned by the incoming tide of another day.

Sula Sgeir disappears astern, a citadel for seabirds hidden in the ocean; the island is abandoned for another year.

Murdo returns home to his job as a weaver; and Stuart travels back to England and, like us all, will never forget his journey to Sula Sgeir.

Against the harbour wall at Port of Ness, the glistening baskets of gugas are lifted
from the hold to be heaped on to the quay.

Local weaver Andy Burns and Angus Murdo's father, Donald, help to lift the baskets of gugas on to the quay. Young and old offer assistance.

There are many hands to help empty the baskets onto the huge pile of gugas growing on the quay.

Early the following morning, the gugas are allocated into equal portions for the men who went to Gannet Rock; this is a time-honoured ceremony. Most birds are sold privately, but a batch is kept for public sale off the quay.

Hundreds of people from Lewis come to see the sale of the gugas, and to buy a pair for themselves. These will be kept preserved or frozen for a special occasion when a guga feast will be prepared.

The gugas are priced this year at £10 a pair, covering a bit more than the cost of hiring the trawler and the cost of supplies.

Kenny Murray's children, Tam and Julie, are intrigued with the pile of gugas.
The quayside is glistening with guga grease.

Veteran guga hunter Murdo Macfarlane, right, recounts some of his adventures on
Sula Sgeir to first-timer Norman Macdonald. The tradition continues.

Dods Macfarlane, the stecly-disciplined and unspoken leader of this year's team, shows the gentle side of his nature to his god-daughter, Julie Murray.

Notes on the Photography ——————————

The task of photographing the incredible story of Sula Sgeir has been an exacting and intimate affair. Without the full co-operation of all the men concerned and their dedicated approval and permission, my work would have been impossible.

During the past ten years, the type of work I've undertaken has led me to this story in a strange sequence of events, and the discipline I learned over that time stood me in good stead, providing the right resources to call on when needed.

The first resource I called up has been nurtured through years of living in extreme conditions whilst photographing in wilderness areas of the world. Mountain bivouacs in the Arctic, Nepal and America; struggling through dark rainswept nights over long-distance walks in Britain, sleeping on beaches, in deserts and the decks of foreign ships, all these experiences helped me to cope with the hardships of life on Sula Sgeir. They visited me like old friends: freezing fingers, insects in the sleeping bag and wet clothes for days on end. To take a photograph that expresses hardship, one must live and feel hardship.

In the past, I have enjoyed photographing the realism and excitement of rock climbing; therefore, I found I could cope with the rock antics and danger of cliff work on Sula Sgeir. The seabird harvest on the cliffs happens with great speed, so flexibility and ease of movement in undoubtedly dangerous situations gave me an opportunity to photograph the action from unusual viewpoints and angles. Perhaps the most testing skill was in attempting to capture a sense of the lives of the men of Sula Sgeir, a fleeting expression, a moment of tension, or a sudden glimpse of a character trait – these are the layers I have searched for, helped by the fact that many of these elements occurred in moments of stress. When the Blondin line collapsed there was unguarded exasperation; during the hunt, fierce action; during the meals there was companionship. The most successful artistic opportunities are rarely the results of being in the right place at the right time; they are a blend of technical discipline and intuitive thinking.

The poor weather conditions on Gannet Rock caused immense problems for photography. Great wind speed was the principal difficulty – the constant buffeting often rendered tripod work useless. Constant rain made lenses distort and mist up, and the salt in the air from sea spray caused untold damage in the cameras' electronics. The low light often meant changing film stock frequently, and I often had to balance the cameras on rucksacks or rocks to catch a sudden image.

The experience of working on Sula Sgeir has been one of observation and a critical test of my expertise to record the story as it unfolded. My cameras were the vital tool of contact with the subject, and the framing of that subject was largely won through spontaneity. Out on Sula Sgeir, I took 2 × Canon T90 cameras, a 20mm, 35–105mm zoom, 80–200mm zoom and 2.8 300mm telephoto with a × 1.4 convertor. I used every lens every day, many times, constantly switching as subject choice changed. For film stock I chose Fuji Velvia 50 asa, Fujichrome 100 asa professional, Fujichrome 400 and 1600 for poor light and Kodak T max black and white stock and a sturdy Manfrotto tripod. In a situation requiring reportage, nature and landscape, portraiture and action photography, my 35mm cameras were infinitely easier to handle than other formats.

A final word is one of thanks again to the men of Ness who lived for two weeks under the scrutiny of my lenses, and to whom I gave little privacy.

John Beatty has travelled to the margins of five continents in search of wild places. His photography is chiefly concerned with the timeless rhythms of the natural environment, its beauty and simplicity, man's place within it, and the complexities of his response to it. He lives with his wife and young family in a small Derbyshire village in a wooded valley which is surrounded by heather moorlands.